The Phoenix Living Poets

THE GARRYOWEN

THE GARRYOWEN

by

ROY McFADDEN

CHATTO AND WINDUS

THE HOGARTH PRESS

1971

Published by
Chatto & Windus Ltd
with the Hogarth Press Ltd
42 William IV Street
London WC2

*

Clarke, Irwin & Co Ltd
Toronto

ISBN 0 7011 1764 8

Distributed in the United States of America
by Wesleyan University Press

ISBN: 0 8195 7036 2

Printed in Great Britain by
Lewis Reprints Limited
London and Tonbridge

Contents

Acknowledgments are made to *The Irish Times; The Dublin Magazine; Irish Writing; Threshold; Outposts; Hibernia; The Irish Press; Truth; New World Writing; The Oxford Book of Irish Verse; The Guinness Book of Poetry; The Best Poems of 1959; New World Writing; The British Broadcasting Corporation:* and to my co-editor of *Rann.*

GLENARM

For Margaret

Nobody told me then—
When I mooned around Portrush in a wet July—
That you, 13, I steeped in my 14 years,
Were in Glenarm:
Scraped girlish legs in ferns; shrilling at sudden sea.

Who could have told me then,
Putting a ball towards a diffident hole,
Skimming skinny flints from the North Strand,
Despising dodgem cars in the brash arcade;
Bored by the boardinghouse, restless, and stretching
Beyond the gulls' complaint, and the finsharp islands
Only a handshake over the waves' last futile fuss—
That if I'd shouted, set a house on fire,
You might have noticed; curious, come to see.

Nobody told me then—
That loneliness is never an only thing;
That sometime somewhere there's an expectant hand,
A tentative harbour for unanchored sea,
And a destination printed in the sand.

I couldn't tell you then—
You in Glenarm, the glens spread like a palm—
Skirting the fuchsias' bells, past rhododrendons and
Moonclad magnolia trees, a haze of bees—
That a boy coasting disaster, aloof on a strand,
Conjured up someone like you in hope of a quick thereafter,
To be known perhaps in a house busy with children singing and
spelling.

INDEPENDENCE

The sun itself was cheering, so they said;
On tiptoe in the sky, shouting hurray:
And all along the hot processional way
Laughter and songs exploded in the street
Where bombs and guns coughed blood the other day.
Dead patriots shuddered under the dancers' feet.

At last he came, his face like a black sun,
Traitor, terrorist, conspirator
Against an empire, now Prime Minister.
Silence hissed like rain as he stepped out
To say it to the straining faces there,
All ready to acclaim it with a shout.

But up there on the platform he looked small
And worn with study, exile, intrigue, jail,
Bewildered by the view inside the pale,
The years of hurt and work behind, the strong
Laws of authority now his to flail
To right or left, defining right and wrong.

And then he couldn't say it. There weren't any
Uncommitted words that could convey
Naked truths for Independence Day.
How could he *say* it when he *was* the thing?
He laughed out loud, and danced down like a gay
Enraptured child still fond enough to sing.

ROGER CASEMENT'S RISING

Good Friday in good Ireland. Risen larks
Soared from his footsteps and created over
His gaunt surprise, arresting place and time,
His journey's end. And made light of the darks

And guttering vicious entries in his mind.
Wet primroses and primfaced violets
All-eyed his watery rising on a strand
Of faceless shells turned from the shoreward wind.

He had no mind, smarting with salt and zeal,
For hired collectors of his private words
Indulgently put down soon to inform
And in the final judgment dock his tale.

Coy flowers, agnostic larks, ran down his fear's
Long spine of disillusion. In the end,
Disowned belongings, longings, quest undressed,
Were dirty linen washed by a priest's tears.

SYNGE IN PARIS

On the Pont de la Concorde, between the mad
Skeltering traffic and the pampered river
Trailing a violet scarf across the town,
He eyed from a jap of shadow, his book turned-down,
The gurgling pleasureboat, the tittering girls
With pouting breasts and skirts fanned-out like shells.
Above, the flag of France, stiff, head-in-air;
And there at his feet, twin leaves in a trance like curls.
But, unimpressed, his brooding foreign mind
Schooled by Irish drizzle, sceptical
Of total sunshine, knuckled like a cloud
Over the city, trained in the ways of the wind,
Remembered flooded fields, breached harbour wall.

POEM FOR JOHN BOYD

The streets are strewn with footprints. There
Yeats walked beneath instructing trees.
Joyce raised his ashplant to confer
A footnote on those sunsprayed quays.
In that dim corner Synge would stare
At naked wall for half-an-hour.

Harsh leaves, the rattling footsteps blow
Across the windy town, and dead
Voices rise in a wave and throw
Salty words on heedless head,
Claiming, declaiming there is no
City outside the dream they knew:

That Ireland is a name they bred
In poem or in hounded play,
That outside exiled words they said
Nothing continues to obey
The dictate of the dream. The dead
Are mercenaries free from blood.

All that you or I can do
Is to perpetuate the dream,
Using each footprint to pursue
The dreamers past that noisy stream
Of printless footsteps stumbling through
Each named but undreamed avenue.

What I wrote in Stephen's Green,
As a sadmouthed boy in a lonely place,
Deaths ago and births between,
Has swung into truth again, found grace,
As the spire's unsleeping cock is seen
Interpreting the storm alone.

MEMORIES OF CHINATOWN

Jackie Dugan

1

Under a streetlamp Jackie Dugan
Whipped his peerie-top alone—
Hoarse from yodelling out faint friends
Tucked up in sleeping houses where
Black grates were set, white tables laid.

His father wore a uniform
Of navyblue with seams piped red,
Heels sparking steel on tramcars' stairs
Where he supported bag and bell.
His mother danced; came home at one.

2

He frightened me, for he was tough
And terse and tearless, unafraid.
He jumped from bedroom window once
Because he wouldn't wear new shoes.
They dragged him home and forced them on.

At Kick-the-can, Relieve-i-o,
He was the master in the ring.
I turned away from bedtime kiss
Each night he yodelled in the street,
Assassin of my innocence.

3

He mocked me, but I don't recall
A hard slap up the bake, or any
Physical outrage. He stood
Outside my world and mocked me. Not

Because of my capped doctored eye
Or my weak stomach, or because
My speech was alien: but because
He lacked my privilege of love.

His mother taxied off to love,
Leaving his bed unmade, his plate
Unscraped; his kissless bedtime prayer
Unheard by skivvy clashing pans.

4

From kitchen's soiled deserted door
Jackie Dugan stayed out late
Hunched in the lamplight, whipping top
With leather thong, intent, alone.

Heels scorched on stone hotwater jar,
I'd lift a guilty ear to catch
His last cracked yodel, and endure
The silent circle, top run dead.

Clutey Gibson's Eviction

Cordner Bell said Clutey Gibson's da
Sold penny pokes of home-made yellowman.
I ran with penny to his scullery where
He shredded *Northern Whig* and tented poke
Around his thumb to drop four pieces in,
Slipping my penny in a pocket where
Fat watch pokes out from real confectioner.

One morning, late for school with piece and bag
Under my arm, I hirpled round a pyre
Of Clutey's chattels dumped against the gate.
My high-heeled sister said that Clutey's da
Piled chairs and bedding on a red handcart
And, Clutey barking heels, humped towards Strandtown.

Bigamy

His cycle kerbed, the peeler found
The lad behind the door, the girl
Biting her flowered pinafore,
Hushed neighbours aching for a sound.

The lad went with the constable,
Cap wedged inside his pocket with
A blackened butt and one red match,
And helped to push the bicycle.

The girl stole in and closed the blinds.
Neighbours stormed to angry pans
And urgent irons' climbing steam,
Straitlaced within their marriage-lines.

But no one chased the constable
To ask what harm the lad had done
In kindling love on her cold hearth;
Or who would be accountable

For her trousseau of cast-off love,
Her honeymoon arrested; shame
Shrouding her presence like a shawl,
Bare thumb betrayed in Sunday glove.

THOSE GLORIOUS TWELFTHS

At ten I saw exclamatory blood
On Earlswood Road, a cagecar and a beak-
Capped constable with crowblack gun. We went
To Portrush in July, the great event
Abstracted to indifferent gull and rock.

At twenty, reading law, I glimpsed a gun
Glint in the smile of D.I., former Tan,
War-hero who'd won fancy ribboned stuff
For gutting Germans. Dead Huns not enough,
He grilled halfbaked dissenting Irishmen.

At thirty, pigmy family nudging knee,
Wedged in a village dazed by roaring drums
That drowned my destination; trapped by tied
Tiers of faces blinding stonedeaf road:
Inactive, voiceless, I chewed famine crumbs

Like those who willed another hopeless day
Eyeing the shrivelled root and the stopped hand.
Now forty, knowing men in government,
And collared curs that bark down argument
And foul what they must fail to understand:

I hurry children from the bloodsmeared drums,
Myself from the Inspector. If I rein
My family back into integrity,
Into a lane that's lamed by a quick tree,
I'll turn a leaf will dock the nettle's pain.

But let me give them one clear argument
Aloof from cheers and flags, like faceless rain:
One unembarrassed guilty monument,
Skirting the queen outside the City Hall,
To smuggle flowers to graves it can't disown.

SHEEPDOG TRIALS

Sheila and Roy and Mick: at Waterfoot
(Remember) they obeyed each whistled call,
Alert to each small signal; the pursuit
And herding in of sheep was gentle, wise
And moving to us watching at the edge.
They won again today the paper says.
And, reading, I remember hill and hedge
Shaggy with rain, the tea and sandwiches
Sold in a corner of the barking field:
And, in the foreground, you embracing him,
The champion, who, tolerant, would yield
Neither to hand nor word, but sat erect
In solitary pride; no, pride is wrong:
In ancient loneliness; yes, gazing out
Across the sheep-pens and the fuchsia hedge,
To where the hills are blurred by thickening cloud.

THE ARCADIA

Old women wading, kilting skirts
Above the slugbunched veins, massage
Embarrassed thighs, and clumsily
Snatch water like a sign across the face.

Younger, they were those coarse loud
Matrons who jested while I wailed
Wet at the edge, their navy skirts
Tucked into knickerlegs, or rudely held

Tumescent over fanning waves'
Screamed-at incursions: breasted-out
Like old ships' figureheads that rode
Disastrous storms they never figured out.

I chide my children to the edge,
Where faint waves shrink from cringing toes.
They fear the claw and the quicksand,
Where I cried shame a hundred fears before.

CONTEMPLATIONS OF MARY

1

When he said *Mary,* she did not at once
Look up to find the voice, but sat recalling
Warm patches of her childhood, and her falling
Heartoverhead in love with every glance
Of admiration crowding through the dance,
Or in the streets bent back and almost calling.

Girls put on sex like flowers; their small breasts
Emerge like blushes, knowing, innocent;
The underflow of all their ways intent
On welling up with welcome for the guests
Who darken love's white threshold. All the rest's
Above, outside, like god and government.

So she sat on when he first spoke to her.
Hearing perhaps a new sound of command,
Like parent's tug at child's reluctant hand,
Did not at once look up and answer *Sir,*
But sat with memory her conspirator,
Downcast, and did not want to understand.

But he persisted. *Mary.* She resigned
Her meadows and her rainbows to his voice,
Inevitably now, without a choice,
Surrendering all the stairways of her mind;
Then, finally bereft, was empty, blind,
Until the word bulged up and broke. *Rejoice.*

Then she was different. Her past perfect years
Seemed like another woman's purse, all strange
In ordinary things, keys, compact, change:
And home no longer nested up those stairs,
Involved with tables, pictures, cupboards, chairs.

Everything was leaning out askew
Since it had touched, no hardly touched her, blown
A strange breath through her branches and the mown
And planted garden of her private view,
Those yesterdays no longer *I* but *you*.

Was it her knowledge of the clouded womb
That crowded out her quiet corridors:
Her certainty of child? Or, like far doors
Slamming goodbyes, was it a shout of doom,
The dying of a world in her small room:

Her mind a skirt of fear ballooning back
To girlish unencumbered days when life
Required no definitions; sweetheart, wife
Made love, embroidered, lived without some lack
Of meaning like a rat at every crack:

Mary, still girl enough to twirl her hood
From birth and death conspiring in her blood
Against the bright truth of her platitude?

After the dying, tidying her room,
She pondered, wondered why he had cried out
In protest for his father. Was his shout
Indictment of the seed that filled her womb
Or plea for some known name to mark his tomb?
Now she was parched and hollowed out with doubt.

She had been satisfied the way things were,
Girl among girls, doing the usual things.
Then she had been exalted, hearing wings
Applauding through the galleries of air;
Came to know words that first had made her stare,
And talk to common people as to kings.

It never was her doing. She had been
Only the bottle for the conjured wine.
Involved with something magic or divine,
She had no axe to grind, no slate to clean,
Had never bothered with a party line.
Most of the things he said she did not mean.

Now she was empty. The last drop had gone,
And she was her own Mary, uninvolved
With parables or politics, resolved
To self, undedicated, pledged to none.
And just before the colours, blurred, dissolved,
She closed the door on her disfigured son.

4

I am the breath that stirred
Your bells to jubilance;
Conjured from cold distance
As surely as a bird
Immense obeisance:
I am the word.

My irresponsible
Dialogue broke down,
Was hooted, hissed and blown
Off stage in ridicule,
My sad forgiving clown
A love-crossed fool.

But I would blow again
My horn into your sleep;
Herd rational thought like sheep
Into a nursery pen;
Scatter my wolves to sweep
Doubt from the plain.

Yes, I would fill your page,
Your lines with poetry:
With liberating key
Empty the clipped lark's cage,
And give back wings to free
Ecstatic rage.

Mary, I am cold,
Bare on the brink of mind.
Open, and let me find
A place to grip and hold,
To thrust the exiled seed
In knowing mould.

FOLKMINDER

For Michael J. Murphy

That time in Cushendall
When sun tompeeped through slatted drizzle at the hills
Stretched like Pegeen Mike or Molly Bloom
Back to the tide's necklace, the wetmouthed *yes* of the sea:
Then birds flashed; and tutting hens fretted past foundering
                                                    gates.
Summer then. Yes, fuchsias set red bonnets at the bees.

That summer in the Glens
When you charmed memory back to chilled shawled minds
Of painbright births, toil, copulation, deaths;
Cleaning aborted streams, you groped for life
For love, for neverafter.
Summer then, quick gossip in the hedges.

What eyes snapped then I mind:
Your lovebright kitchen, glowing glancing children;
Small Winifred asleep, world clutched with doll in pram:
Yourself, burdened with silence, padding roads to poach
A shadowy thought from old polluted stream;
Yourself, goodman at home, inching buckets past
Transparent dream, her waterpale limp palm.

NIGHT FISHING: CUSHENDALL

They drag the hidden net towards the shore
Nervous with shadows and grey staring stones,
The village voiceless under a single star,
A full sea dozing over burnished bones,
Plotting the morning murder of the shore.

The far boat creaks an oar, and a voice falls
Faint from the distance, calls, and veers to sea.
Abrupt lines tighten, strain; and life explodes
In manacles and miracles, still free
To ride the net with rainbow waterfalls.

Life against life. I walk into the dark,
Angling a voice in this night-netted town;
Breaking silence underfoot like glass:
Tongued with stones and fishes crying down
Abandoned streets and avenues of dark.

FAMILY ALBUM

ONE

Trespasser

May the small resolute shoes that guard the bed
Of my young son (intent in sleep) resist
No act of trespass for threats on a board.
Yet let them train those wild emphatic feet
To pass the prohibitions on the lawns
Of clipped conformity, the private roads
Shaded from history, the watchdog walls
Roaming the boundaries of the proud demesne:
Not putting heel where toe is for the sake
Of outraging the gamekeepers; but no,
Permit him, in his time, to walk straight on
To where the last forbidding sign says Stop,
At the map's edge; for there he'll comprehend
The final prohibitions, penalties
Of ultimate disaster. In the high
Air where all alternatives are clear,
He'll find the will to choose: to throw the map
And compass far behind and stride across
The line that shapes life, also islands, lives;
Or else to turn, with equal freedom, back
Down to the city, carrying his love
A broken bird snatched from the end of the world.

Forebears

If you were to ask *Where are they,*
Those sunlit faces cornered in the album,
Kin I have never seen, who stumble through your stories?—
What should I say to your three alertly insistent years?

—That they were like us once, walked the same roads we travel,
touched

Those chairs, that table, wound that loitering clock:
And always chose, preferred, the longer
Minatory lanes to the secure and sane
Highways of coming and going allied to things trusted and
dusted,
That never show knuckles like snarls but suggest handshakes
and flowers:

Evading the terrible answer that they
Are all and nothing, night perhaps to your day.

Children's Hospital

Because you are not here,
With your seven years, your need to know,
Your flattening curls, your new big stranger's teeth,
Thought-threatened forehead, life a watched bird in your
hands—
Because you are not here,
I think of all the absences I've known,
The distances, the listenings,
And speculate on your inheritance:
Sadness, nostalgia, shadowy revolt.
My son, be no man's son and no son's father;
But stand against the sun, throw down your shadow.
And, in the meantime, hands and deeds curled, sleep.
Tomorrow is too soon, for yesterday's
A flat cracked photograph without a date,
And your horizons still are packed with sheep
And peeping shepherdesses telling tales.
—Sleep, unsuspecting surgeon's mask and knife.
Too soon, my son, there's no escape from life.
The sheep are slaughtered. Innocence must die.
You must grow to be you, as I, God knows, am I.

TWO

Feis

1

My small taut daughter on the stage,
Pink-eared, braved auditorium.
Behind a pillar, I could gauge
Little of how she had engaged
Adjudicator shredding thumb.

2

Her class came fourth. She was annoyed.
Behind my pillar I contained
The silent watcher, her forced words;
Sharing a pink girl's broken joy
With paid professional restraint.

3

Too soon she'll put on adult dress
And mime the mediocrity
That affluence breeds in fake outrage;
Disowning what was washed and blessed
In modesty for grief and praise.

4

A girl once told me in her shame
Her dying father took the dole.
Behind the pillar my banked name
Sprayed no flowers for my daughter. Lamed
By greater griefs, I patched my soul,
And tholed the judge's shredded down-turned
                                        thumb.

Afternoon

Looking at a snapshot of me, 8
Years-old or so, my daughter sees her brother.
And I whose childhood is a story to her
Ponder the far-off childhood of my mother
Run in another country with strange names.

The years queue up behind me this June day.
Uneasy in the sunshine I turn heel
To tease tense out of history, sense from play,
Now actor without audience, playwright
Without a theatre, singer without songs.

I tell her she is wrong; that boy grew up:
Her brother still plays games of right and wrong,
His sun and shadows slanting from outside.
Dismayed survivor of that eight-year-old,
I rein the impulse to go running back
Into the photograph, and stoop to scold
A little girl for dancing on my grave
Deliberations, when I could step out
And take her clouds and rainbows in my hand
And, eight years old, pursue life with a shout.

THREE

Grania At Three

1

Eager, querulous to be understood
In a world of table-talk, you primly walk
Out with grandfather under elderly trees,
Chatting and chuckling with your leaves and birds,
Embracing clouds and windows lit with sun.
And now and then you dance around a tree,
Or chase a dwindling leaf, because you must
Run for dear life, knowing *to be* is free.

28

That gaelic Grania was a flighty girl
That made an old king conscious of his heart,
And ran a boily boy into his grave.
But what have you to do with myth and moth?
Your present —(my gift)— soon, yourself aghast,
Will fade in family album with the past.
But now your small scuffed shoes dance round a tree
Anxious and friendly like your grandfather
Who, contemplating ivy, lets you be.

FOUR

Taurus

Bull-like you charge. Then, swung up in my arm,
You turn your golden head, and smile, and charm
The pictures off the walls. If I must brake
Your bullrush for the china, don't mistake,
My Christy-Mahon angry smiley boy,
The owing for the ruing, Owen Roy.

FIVE

Antenatal

Upstairs the baby quarrels in the womb.
The others are asleep, clenched, or abandoned
To skeltering funfair dream. Outside the room
A wind probes at the door like some forgotten
Father late for feast or funeral.
The wounded blackbird eyes its feathers fall.

What will it be, slow clock, a son or daughter?
Who cares, if it has four limbs and a head:
Cool eyes, hot heart, and the flint of ironic laughter
Equating crust of sin with holy bread.
The blackbird silhouettes a stony head.

Changer of nappies, god's lap, endless hands:
Let this brash ignorant child that dares presume
To stumble into a world where reason stands
Aghast at disaster or promised disaster, exhume
A laughing blackbird from the window's gloom.

Sing like a blackbird shawled on a white thorn
For every child striped like a refugee.
If death is a neverafter, then be born
With a late agnostic breath, death's enemy,
As the crippled blackbird sings, outraged and free.

The outraged blackbird sings. Stripped refugee,
A child knocks at the door, shrill girl, gruff son,
Careless of name and nationality,
Eager for the journey to be done.
The crippled blackbird summons, its song done.

SIX

Probate

One hardfaced January day
My father walked out to his death;
Fell on the street like tagless stray
Cat or dog caught up beneath
Late scheduled wheels; stumbled, and left

His papers tidy, his affairs
Ready for probate. Son bereft,
(Suddenly father) he confers
On me his pipes and walking sticks,
That birthday scarf, the hats too small,
My mother's papers. Now I'll fix
Fuses, wind slow clocks, and call
On frayed relations, tend the grave,
Press speeches for occasions, stay

To hear pink chubby clichés pave
The road to hell or Stormont: pray.

Old God of lamplight, do not hold
Him guilty of his son; but let
Him enter heaven was foretold
By old believers. I would not,
To save myself like Joyce, have said
One word against survival, that
Sole meaning for the decent dead.
No, I would kneel and crumple hat
And cancel out myself for that.

Cold air, sweet dissolution, in the spring
Grania, threeyearsold, remembering
His presence with last Easter's egg,
Will stray on silence that will beg
The honest questions she'll prefer.

If I inherit, who'll confer?

Bereft, perplexed, a child and I
Follow a window's curt goodbye,
And sudden death calls casual life
To wipe death off a kitchen knife.

Lacking a brief for life, I will
Indict the indefensible.

Last Christmas

Christmas night. Full cars storm home.
Glutted with fowl and fun I close
On pinched moon and quenched houses door
That admits and denies.

Last Christmas day my father picked
A slippered way through tumbled toys
And scrambling children, praised the fowl,
And lipped his final glass.

How do you tell a child to mourn
On Christmas day except to say
From small cribs adult crosses grow:
God dies with each good day.

Unfathered father at son's feast
I close the door on Son's first day,
My father's last good day, to learn
His skills gleaned by the way:

Wrist plying crafty screwdriver,
Foot and hand behind a spade.
I bring to manger murder and
A craftsman slabbed and dead.

Christmas night. Cars screwdrive home.
The child is born, the father dies.
A door jambed on eternity
Permits, admits, denies.

THE GARRYOWEN

A Soldier's Song; the silence: then the roar
Of Lansdowne-Irish voices. (Who reflects
On Morgan, Cromey, Bailey, Moran, Kyle,
And Sammy Walker and Blair Mayne? The score
Will be forgotten in a little while).
Stopped on the line, O'Reilly genuflects.

Crumpled packs dishevel holy ground,
While fledgling wings inch forward for a sign.
In forced tumescent waves the faceless crowd
Washes the field with sublimating sound;
Implores, deplores, ejaculates aloud.
On, up and under, forwards. Charge the line.

Irish for an afternoon they wait
For gory glory-o, the faceless men.
Close men from Belfast, Ballymena, loud
As Dubliners, uncorked men, imprecate
Together in some sort of brotherhood.
Mothproofed, the old myths stagger out again.

The ball hangs like a sighted bird, and falls.
Lost causes charge the packed imperial mass.
While clockfaced Fate chimes destiny from time,
Who looks through game to life; hears ashblown calls:
Sees shamrock-favours bloom to clouds that climb
Above the cancelled world that missed the pass?

The symbol dominates and germinates.
Ball shamrocks like a bomb; the partisan
Applause gasps like the last transparent tree.
(Look, there's MacNeice the poet who relates
While Moffett squares up to the penalty
Morgan and Cromey, Bailey, Kyle, Moran).

33

The barking journalists lift pints and vet
Past victories and defeats. In Davy Byrne's
The Belfast men with club conformist ties
Buy quick ones, nationality, and rate
Moffett and Mulligan, free kicks and tries.
Short of the line an offside bomber turns.

Let's talk of Championship and Triple Crown,
But not forget in toasting victory
What the final shout will be about.
Before you put the sporting record down,
Ponder and Irish remedy for rout:
The Garryowen, and the game set free.

BRENDAN BEHAN

A broth of an Irish boy no doubt
But Joyce be with us, don't neglect
The learning or the intellect,
His knowing what he was about.

He died in headlines, for he turned
Away from one man's private death;
The air he breathed was public breath.
Perhaps because he'd death discerned

He chose to play the roaring boy
Before the faceless firing-squad;
To hound his words against the broad
Backside of ambiguity.

Some pace their lives. But he outran
Detective and health visitor,
Conformity with clichés, where
Civility puts drawers on Pan.

They'll say his drouth drank him to death
With Dylan Thomas. Who's to say
What impulse prodded them to pray
At altars that required their death?

If I prepare an elegy
For big gay heads reduced to bone:
Alerted, briefed, I face my own
Undoing in sobriety.

SECOND LETTER TO AN IRISH NOVELIST

For Michael McLaverty

Yourself unchanged, shy habits undisturbed:
After twenty years you still wring change
Out of skint purse of knuckled payerspent hands,
And fondle story's detail, poem's phrase,
As farmer claps a beast or rubs ripe grain—
Because from ink and clabber they've come through.

Still *Sons and Lovers* you evaluate
The major novel of this century,
As when we first talked in a dying war.
But now I don't read Lawrence any more,
My favourite book a street directory
That pages streets forever running home.

How to escape from a parenthesis
Back to the narrative and argument
Is not solely a novelist's concern.
I file at words like keys that might unlock
A sentence from curt brackets' manacles,
A present tense from phrase's culdesac.

On early breathgrey mornings you walk out
And finger frost, note cuckoospit and drawn
Threads in the hedges, introverted trees:
Then, at the altar, hear unaltering word
That needs no key or confidential file,
No laddering wall or jarred heel's certainty.

I travail over clabbered clout of ground
Whose sanction's not imposed but must be worked
Up from graves with delf and bone and snarl;
And riddle shard and soil, and scrabble for

Absolving evidence for cornered god
Thorned in the hedges, hung in decadent trees.

If, unabridged, we fish in the same stream,
You go to mass, I walk doomed heelbright streets,
Squinting at dates on buildings, searching for
The architect behind a boarded door;
Evicted tenants in demolished streets
Who served their sentence in parenthesis.

THE GOLDEN BOY

That time John Kennedy came home
To death-kiss of the Irishry,
Cuchulainn quit a hero's tomb
Rifled by mythology.

First, because he was a man
A late First Lady and her two
Knee-squiring children craned to scan
Long lines of grief beyond review.

Because he was the President
They mourn a necessary man.
—Inquiring children, answered wife:
Authority taught hands to train

Gun on a face that watched for life;
Unmasked an intellectual thought
For purchased gun to mark it down.
Disarmed by reason he was shot

Because he was the president
It was his own authority
That armed the hands that mailed the gun
That tore him out of history.

That time John Kennedy came home
To death-myth of the Irishry,
To wish and moth of martyrdom,
Life settled for mythology.

IN DRUMCLIFFE CHURCHYARD

If that old man had clambered from the hearse,
How many could have said they'd read his verse
With more than the cold glancing of an eye:—
That hardfaced mourner from the Ministry?
That poet drooling for the next review?
They might have felt an irate poet's shoe
Applied abruptly to posterity,
And heard the voice that mauled authority
In play and speech before rant from the dead
At drunkards putting sober men to bed.
In Drumcliffe Churchyard they obey today,
Bringing a skeleton to Irish clay
For Irish worms to pick at. But he'll write
His signature elsewhere, beyond the trite
Observances of country and of creed;
Endorse the tree on which Cuchulainn died.

PREMONITION

I can never be alone again.
Here now, in the silence, I can sense
The prowling dog of loneliness slouch past
From room to hall, rousing a restless ring
Of questions like the winter's whingeing leaves.
I say lie still, or open doors to find
Always before me sad and questioning eyes,
Stairways of restless feet stitching the dark,
The heart a clock regretting its lost chime.

THE SUMMER'S GONE

Regretfully I say goodbye to Cushendall:
To the tree-thatched road that marries sea and sky,
The minding hills, and the sudden sun-smeared morning mists
                                    that scrawl
Child-signatures across a schoolbook sky,
Loanens that rear like kicking horses, and the hard
Cough of crow and creak of the cold unminding gull.

Bereft on a hill of thought, nostalgic, I regard
The shoresweep of my days in Cushendall;
And, at my desk, snatch suddenly at smell and sound,
Blown truant scraps through a lazy gap in the wind,
And wish for turf under my feet and all around
Infinity of cold and heartless wind.